Lev~~el~~ **1** ~~ived~~

some ~~told,~~
or su~~b~~ ~~a small~~
numb

Spec~~ial features:~~

Dinosaur words

Triceratops
(Try-SERRA-tops)

meat

plants

Diplodocus
(DIP-low-DOCK-us)

teeth

Tyrannosaurus rex
(Tie-RAN-oh-sore-us rex)

Velociraptor
(Vel-OSS-ee-rap-tor)

8
9

Opening pages
introduce key
subject words

A long, long time ago

Dinosaurs lived here a long,
long time ago.

The dinosaurs are not
here now.

Careful match
between text
and pictures

All these dinosaurs lived
here a very long time ago.

Large, clear labels and captions

Educational Consultant: Geraldine Taylor

Book Banding Consultant: Kate Ruttle

LADYBIRD BOOKS

UK | USA | Canada | Ireland | Australia
India | New Zealand | South Africa

Ladybird Books is part of the Penguin Random House group of companies
whose addresses can be found at global.penguinrandomhouse.com.

ladybird.com

First published 2015
002

Copyright © Ladybird Books Ltd, 2015

Ladybird, Read it yourself and the Ladybird logo are registered or
unregistered trademarks owned by Ladybird Books Ltd

The moral right of the author and illustrator has been asserted

Printed in China

A CIP catalogue record for this book is available from the British Library

ISBN: 978-0-723-29507-5

Dinosaurs

Written by Catherine Baker

Illustrated by Mike Spoor

Contents

Dinosaur words

Triceratops
(Try-SERRA-tops)

meat

plants

8

Diplodocus
(DIP-low-DOCK-us)

teeth

Tyrannosaurus rex
(Tie-RAN-oh-sore-us rex)

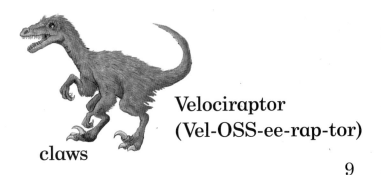

Velociraptor
(Vel-OSS-ee-rap-tor)

claws

9

A long, long time ago

Dinosaurs lived here a long, long time ago.

The dinosaurs are not here now.

All these dinosaurs lived
here a very long time ago.

Plants

Some dinosaurs liked plants.

plant

Triceratops

Triceratops was a big dinosaur
that liked plants very much.

13

Meat

Some dinosaurs liked meat. Tyrannosaurus rex was a strong dinosaur that liked meat very much.

Triceratops

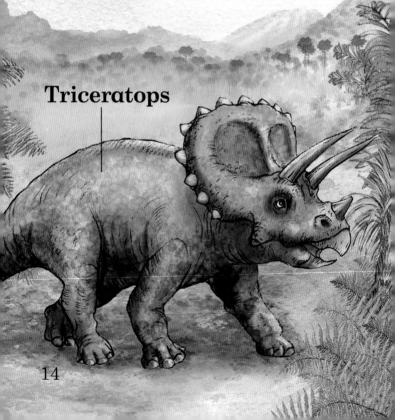

Tyrannosaurus rex

meat

Look out, Triceratops!
Tyrannosaurus rex likes meat! 15

Little dinosaurs

Many dinosaurs were
very little.

Velociraptor

Velociraptor was a little dinosaur.
It liked meat, too.

Big dinosaurs

Some dinosaurs were very big.

Diplodocus was a very, VERY big dinosaur!

Diplodocus

Diplodocus liked plants
like these.

Strong teeth

Some dinosaurs had big, strong teeth.

Tyrannosaurus rex had teeth that were VERY big and strong.

Tyrannosaurus rex

teeth

Look out! Tyrannosaurus rex's teeth
are VERY big!

Big claws

Some dinosaurs had big claws.

Velociraptor had VERY big, strong claws!

Velociraptor

Look at the Velociraptor's
BIG claws.

claws

23

Strong dinosaurs

Some dinosaurs were very strong.

Diplodocus was very big and strong.

Diplodocus

Tyrannosaurus rex was not as big as Diplodocus, but it was very strong.

Look at Tyrannosaurus rex's strong teeth.

Dinosaurs now

Come in here to see
dinosaurs now!

You can see many, many dinosaurs in here!

Picture glossary

 claws

 Diplodocus

 meat

 plants

 teeth

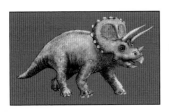 Triceratops

 Tyrannosaurus rex

 Velociraptor

Index